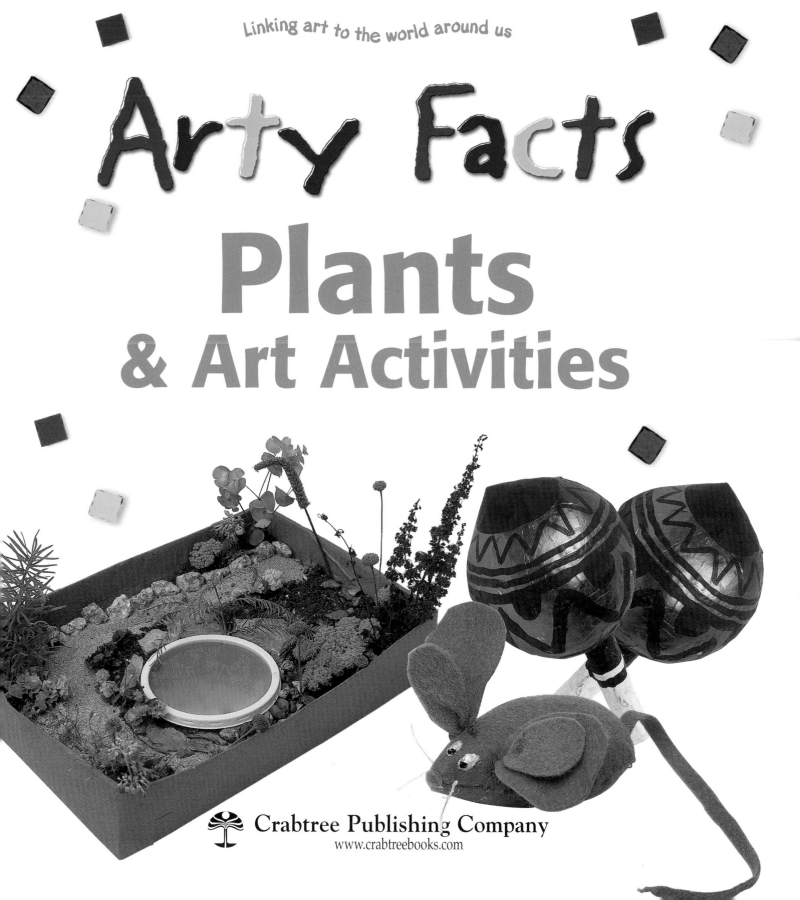

Linking art to the world around us

Arty Facts

Plants
& Art Activities

Crabtree Publishing Company
www.crabtreebooks.com

Crabtree Publishing Company

PMB 16A, 350 Fifth Avenue, Suite 3308
New York, NY
10118

612 Welland Avenue
St. Catharines, Ontario
L2M 5V6

Coordinating Editor: Ellen Rodger
Project Editors: P.A. Finlay, Carrie Gleason
Production Coordinator: Rosie Gowsell
Proofreading, Indexing: Wendy Scavuzzo

Project Development and Concept Marshall Direct:
Editorial Project Director: Karen Foster
Editors: Claire Sippi, Hazel Songhurst, Samantha Sweeney
Researchers: Gerry Bailey, Alec Edgington
Design Director: Tracy Carrington
Designers: Claire Penny, Paul Montague,
James Thompson, Mark Dempsey,
Production: Victoria Grimsell, Christina Brown
Photo Research: Andrea Sadler
Illustrator: Jan Smith
Model Artists: Sophie Dean,

Prepress, printing and binding by Worzalla Publishing Company

McCormick, Rosie.
    Plants and art activities / Rosie McCormick.
        p. cm. -- (Arty facts)
Includes index.
    Summary: Information about various topics related to petals, tree bark, seeds, and other special characteristics of different plants forms the foundation for a variety of craft projects.
    ISBN 0-7787-1138-2 (paper) -- ISBN 0-7787-1110-2 (rlb.)
        Plants--Juvenile literature. 2. Plants--Study and teaching (Elementary)--Activity programs. [1. Plants. 2. Handicraft.] I. Title. II. Series.
    QK49 .M47 2002
    580--dc21   2002019259
                                                            LC

Created by
Marshall Direct Learning

© 2002 Marshall Direct Learning

Linking art to the world around us

Arty Facts

Plants

& Art Activities

Contents

Leaves	4	Tree nurseries	28
Caps and stalks	6	Hardy plants	30
Woody skin	8	Vegetables	32
Fields of gold	10	Paper and pulp	34
Sprouting seeds	12	Dropping leaves	36
Dwarf trees	14	Exploding spores	38
Tropical beauties	16	Wings and pods	40
Gum and sap	18	Medicinal plants	42
Opening petals	20	Amazing plants	44
Plant juice	22	Glossary	46
Circles of time	24	Index	47
Fancy fossils	26	Materials guide	48

WRITTEN BY Rosie McCormick

Leaves

Leaves produce their own food. They change sunlight, water, and **carbon dioxide** into food to help the plant grow. The leaves of different plants vary in shape, size, texture, and pattern.

Chloroplasts

The leaves of most plants are green. This is because their **cells** contain tiny green parts called **chloroplasts**. Each chloroplast contains a green substance called **chlorophyll**.

Photosynthesis

The chloroplasts use sunlight, carbon dioxide, and water to make food. Sunlight enters the leaf through its clear outer cells. Water reaches the leaf by traveling from the soil up through the roots and stem of the plant. Air, which contains the gas carbon dioxide, enters the leaf through tiny openings in the leaf's surface called **stomata**. Inside the chloroplasts, the chlorophyll uses the energy from the sunlight to combine the water and carbon dioxide and change them into sugars. This process is called **photosynthesis**. The sugars are then turned into **starch**. Tiny pieces of starch are stored in the cells of the leaf and used as food.

Falling leaves

In autumn, the leaves of **deciduous** trees start to die. They change color from green to yellow, red, or brown before falling to the ground. Trees that keep their green leaves all year are called **evergreens**.

Plants

Leaf print patterns

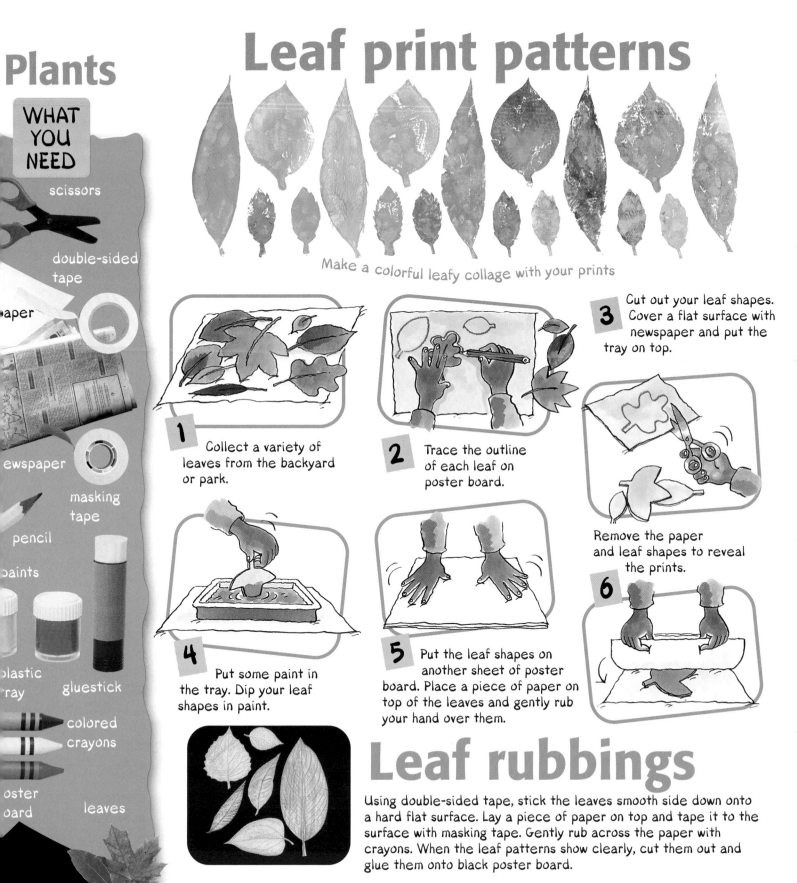

Make a colorful leafy collage with your prints

1 Collect a variety of leaves from the backyard or park.

2 Trace the outline of each leaf on poster board.

3 Cut out your leaf shapes. Cover a flat surface with newspaper and put the tray on top.

Remove the paper and leaf shapes to reveal the prints.

4 Put some paint in the tray. Dip your leaf shapes in paint.

5 Put the leaf shapes on another sheet of poster board. Place a piece of paper on top of the leaves and gently rub your hand over them.

6

Leaf rubbings

Using double-sided tape, stick the leaves smooth side down onto a hard flat surface. Lay a piece of paper on top and tape it to the surface with masking tape. Gently rub across the paper with crayons. When the leaf patterns show clearly, cut them out and glue them onto black poster board.

5

Caps and stalks

Fungi live in damp dark places where most green plants cannot grow. They get their **nutrients** from living things or rotting plants, using their long thin feeding threads that are hidden in the ground. The parts of fungi you can see, such as the caps and stalks of toadstools and mushrooms, come in amazing shapes, sizes, and colors. These parts can be smaller than the tip of a needle or bigger than a watermelon.

Anything but green

Fungi are many different colors. Some are bright orange, such as the fly agaric toadstool, others are silvery-gray, such as the delicate puffball. Fungi are rarely green because they do not contain chlorophyll, the green **pigment** that plants use to make food from sunlight.

Puffballs

Fungi produce **spores** that grow into new fungi. A spore is like a seed, but smaller. Spores grow in the fragile walls, called gills, beneath the umbrella-shape top, or cap, of a mushroom. Puffball spores develop inside a bag-like chamber. If a raindrop gently falls on a puffball, a little cloud of spores puffs out of a tiny hole. Most fungi release their spores into the air. The spores are light, so they can travel a long way. When a spore lands, it grows into a new fungus.

Fairy rings

A fairy ring is a small group of mushrooms growing in a circle in a field or grassy area. Although it is made up of separate mushrooms, they are all part of the same fungus. People once believed fairies created these rings, because they look so magical.

Mushroom or toadstool?

Mushrooms are **edible,** but toadstools are poisonous. Never touch or eat wild fungi because they may be poisonous!

Plants

You can print a masterpiece with mushrooms!

WHAT YOU NEED

mushrooms

paper

paints and brush

colored poster board

glue

1 Ask an adult to cut a mushroom in half. Leave caps on the others, but cut off their stems.

2 Paint the cut surfaces of the mushrooms.

3 Press them down onto your paper to make a print.

4 Create different patterns and mount your finished pictures on colored poster board.

7

Woody skin

This fly trapped in amber is about 40 million years old!

Did you know that trees have skin? Bark is the outer layer of a tree or woody plant and, like your skin, its job is to protect all the parts inside. As a tree grows, it gets too big for its outer skin, so the bark cracks, breaks, and peels off, revealing another layer underneath.

Thin or thick-skinned?

Bark is made up of inner and outer layers. The inner layer is called the **cambium**. It is made up of millions of cells that are continually dividing. When these cells die, they become bark. Every year a new layer of bark is produced and the older layer is pushed to the outside. The bark of a tree can be as thin as two-fifths of an inch (1 cm) or as thick as twelve inches (30 cm).

Tree watching

All plants need the gases **oxygen** and carbon dioxide. They breathe in and out through their trunks as well as their leaves. Examine the bark of a tree to see if you can spot the breathing holes, or **lenticels**.

Made by bark

Cinnamon is a **spice** that comes from the bark of certain types of trees that grow in India and Sri Lanka. To make cinnamon, the bark is cut off these young trees and then left to dry. Cork is the bark of the cork oak tree. About every ten years, the outer layer of bark is stripped away to leave the cambium. Cork is used to make items such as bottle corks, shoes, and furniture.

Clue to the past

Occasionally, nature allows us to glimpse the distant past by providing us with clues of its very own making. When tree trunks are damaged, a substance called **resin** oozes out to protect the wound. Insects sometimes become stuck in the resin. **Fossilized** resin is called **amber**.

Plants

WHAT YOU NEED

paper

poster board

crayons

glue

paints and brush

Bark rubbings

1 Place paper over the bark of a tree and gently rub with a crayon.

2 Make rubbings of the bark from different kinds of trees.

3 Glue your rubbings onto poster board.

Tree rubbings produce surprising patterns to brighten up your wall!

You can paint grainy tree-bark pictures too.

9

Fields of gold

If you were to fly above the vast rolling plains of North America, Russia, or Australia on a warm summer day, you would look down on an endless carpet of gold. These areas grow most of the world's **cereal** crops, such as wheat, barley, corn, rice, oats, and rye, in fields hundreds of times bigger than a football stadium.

Breakfast cereal

Cereals are grasses and we eat their seeds. Wheat is one of the most important cereal crops in the world. It is eaten every day, in some form or another, by more than one third of the world. We grow wheat to make bread, pasta, breakfast cereals, cakes, and cookies.

Feeding the world

Rice is the main food for half the world – more than three billion people. About 90 per cent of the world's rice is grown in Asia. It is grown in **paddies**, which are special fields flooded with water for growing rice.

Amazing maize

In steamy hot subtropical parts of the world, such as Central America, South America, and Africa, the main food is maize, or sweet corn. The corn can be ground into a type of flour called cornmeal, or eaten as a vegetable. It comes in an amazing variety of colors, as well as speckles, spots, and stripes.

Helping the land

The world's fertile farmland must be worked very hard to feed the planet's growing population. The same crops are planted year after year on an enormous scale, over thousands of acres of farm land. This causes the soil to eventually lose its nutrients. As well animals rarely graze on the land now, denying the soil of the nutrients found in the animal dung. Today, chemical **fertilizers** are used to provide nutrients to the soil instead. Many farmers are trying to return to age-old farming methods, such as resting their fields for a year or two to allow the soil to recover. More and more farmers are trying to grow crops without the aid of harmful chemical fertilizers.

Rice-stuffed toys

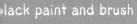

1 Fill a small plastic bag with rice and tie a knot at the end.

2 Cut three red felt ovals, each one slightly bigger than the bag of rice.

3 Sew two ovals together with the bag inside.

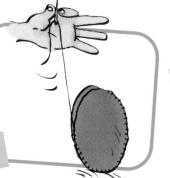

4 Cut six small strips of red felt and sew onto the bottom for the legs.

5 Use the third oval for the wings by cutting it in half and sewing it onto the top of the body.

6 Paint or draw eyes and black spots onto the felt.

Soft felt animals make perfect presents!

Make a mouse using two ovals of blue or gray felt. Sew on ears, whiskers, and a tail.

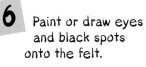

11

Sprouting seeds

It seems amazing that a tree can grow from a tiny seed. Even though most seeds are small, there is a lot packed inside. There is a new plant and a supply of food to help it grow, all wrapped in a tough outer coat. Most seeds are produced by flowers and are contained in fruits, such as tomatoes, oranges, or apples.

Leaving home

Plant seeds of different shapes, sizes, and colors are transported away from their parent plant by the wind, rain, and a variety of animals. If the seeds reach a spot where there is enough space, sunlight, water, and nutrients, then they will start to grow, or **germinate**. In places where there are warm summers and cold winters, plant seeds that are released at the end of the summer wait until spring to grow. This way, they avoid the cold winter months.

Growing up

When a seed has found a suitable place to grow, a root breaks out of the seed coat and starts to take in water and **minerals** from the soil. Then, a shoot pushes up through the soil toward the air and sunlight. Tiny leaves start to grow and begin to make their own food using carbon dioxide, water, and sunlight. The seed's job is done. The young plant now makes its own food. Some seedlings are so strong they can even push their way up toward the sunlight through hard surfaces, such as pavement.

Record holders

The length of time seeds can live without germinating varies. Seeds from willow trees survive for just a few days. The seeds of some weeds can live for almost 50 years. The champion seed is definitely the Arctic Lupin. Ten-thousand-year-old lupin seeds have germinated when given sunlight and water.

When a young plant, such as this one, grows from a seed, it is called a seedling.

Plants

WHAT YOU NEED

paints and brush

paste

toilet paper rolls

sequins

newspaper

rice

tin cans

balloons

cardboard

scissors

tape

Maracas

1 Blow up two balloons.

2 Tear strips of newspaper and paste over the balloons. Leave to dry.

3 Cut the toilet paper rolls and tape into tighter rolls.

Make a hole in the top of the maracas and put in some rice. Push the toilet paper roll into the hole.

5 Paste strips of newspaper around the rolls as shown.

4

6 When dry, paint your maracas.

Now get together with friends and make music!

Shakers

Tear strips of newspaper and paste them over the sides of the two tin cans. Cut two circles out of cardboard to fit over the open ends. Pour rice into the tin cans and then glue the circle tops on. Paint your shakers in bright colors and decorate by gluing on sequins.

Dwarf trees

Over a thousand years ago, people in China and Japan began to show their respect for nature by creating tiny replicas of trees and other plants. Their aim was to create miniature forests and other natural landscapes. They grew these small plants in trays, so the art became known as **bonsai**, meaning tray-planted. By the nineteenth century, bonsai was popular in Japanese homes. Today, the interest has spread to countries worldwide.

Tiny replicas

Most bonsai trees can be between two inches (5 cm) and two feet (.6 m) tall. They are grown to look as much like a full-size tree as possible. Usually, bonsais with small leaves are grown. These include evergreens, such as cedar, pine, and juniper, as well as fruit and flowering trees, such as plum, cherry, and maple. Bonsais can be shaped from young trees or grown from seedlings. They can also be cut from their natural **habitat** when they are small and then planted in containers.

Time and patience

Bonsai growers have a lot of patience, time, and skill. They keep the trees small by re-potting them often and constantly trimming the roots and branches. The size of the pot affects the size of the tree - the smaller the pot, the less the tree will grow. Shape and size are controlled by pinching off new growth, bending the trunk and branches, and using wire to train the plants to grow in a certain shape or direction. The trees stay healthy by careful watering and fertilizing. Bonsai trees can live for hundreds of years.

Plants

cellophane

cardboard box

paints

sand

pebbles

small plants

soil

paintbrush

shallow plastic lid

Miniature garden

Create a fabulous portable garden without even going outdoors!

1 Paint your box in bright colors. Line it with a piece of cellophane.

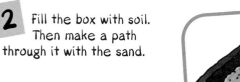

2 Fill the box with soil. Then make a path through it with the sand.

3 Use a plastic lid for a pond. Place pebbles around the outside of your garden and along the sides of the sandy path.

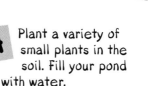

4 Plant a variety of small plants in the soil. Fill your pond with water.

Make sure you water your garden regularly. Plants need damp soil to grow.

Tropical beauties

Wonderfully scented and richly colored orchids are among the most beautiful and unusual flowers in the world. Some are shaped like bees, some grow high up in trees, and some feed on fungus.

There are thousands of kinds of orchids growing all over the world. They are found in large numbers in tropical rainforests.

Growing together

Orchids can grow in soil, as well as on other plants. Wind-**pollinating** varieties of orchids grow on tree trunks. The wind carries the dust-like seeds through the steamy tropical forest air. Many of these seeds fall onto tree trunks where they become attached to the bark. Some orchids cannot make their own food, so they live on dead **organic** matter or are fed by a fungus living in their roots instead.

Pollination tricks

Orchids have developed tricks to make sure that insects and birds carry pollen from one flower to another. Some have an incredible scent that attracts all kinds of eager animals. Others, such as the bee orchid, look like female bees. As a result, male bees try to mate with them and in doing so, carry the **pollen** between the flowers.

Vanilla flavor

Vanilla is a flavoring that is used in baking. It comes from the seeds of several species of orchids.

Plants

Fan orchids

1 Fold the newspaper, tissue paper, and white paper into fans.

2 Draw a flower on the front of each fan and cut it out. Do not cut along the folded edge.

3 Unfold your fan flowers and glue them on colored paper.

You can use all kinds of textured and patterned paper - even comics!

Gum and sap

Look around your home, especially the kitchen, garden, and garage for items made from a material called rubber. The tires on your bicycle, some of the balls you play with, rubber gloves, and elastic bands are all made from rubber.

Collecting rubber

Most of the world's natural rubber comes from rubber trees grown in Asia in special areas called **plantations**. Rubber is the gummy sap of the rubber tree. It is collected by a process called tapping. To tap a tree, a cut is made in the bark and a small tube is inserted. Then, the white milky liquid known as **latex**, that circulates through small veins in the inner bark of the rubber tree, oozes out into a cup. Since the early 20th century, the main source of natural rubber has been the Brazilian rubber tree. It is a tall softwood tree with high wide branches and a large area of bark. The trees are planted in rows on rubber plantations that cover large areas of land in Indonesia, Malaysia, Thailand, India, Vietnam, and Sri Lanka.

Making rubber

After the latex is collected, it is softened by passing it between large rollers or rotating blades. Then, it is mixed with other chemicals to strengthen and stiffen it, so that it can withstand heat and cold. Finally, it is pressed into large sheets. The sheets are cut, shaped, and sold as rubber to factories around the world.

To collect rubber from trees, the tree is tapped.

Rubber band harp

ewspaper

paints and brush

ardboard

sequins

itter

paper towel roll

rubber bands

glue

cissors

1 Cut the paper towel roll, as shown. Cut a circular piece of cardboard to glue on one end.

2 Cut the rubber bands in half and glue them from one end of the roll to the other.

3 Make the frame from cardboard pieces, as shown. Glue it around the tube.

4 Glue strips of newspaper to the frame. When the glue is dry, paint your harp.

5 Decorate with sequins and glitter.

Twang the strings and have fun making music!

19

Opening petals

Have you ever wondered why flowers come in so many different colors, shapes, and types? Or why they smell so nice? Flowers have vibrant colors and beautiful smells in order to attract insects, birds, and other small animals. These visitors ensure that pollen is transferred from one plant to another.

All about pollination

The main job of a plant is to produce seeds that will grow into new plants. For this to happen, a fine powder called pollen from the male part of a flower, the **stamen**, must be transferred to the female part of another flower, the **stigma**. This process is called pollination. Animals, insects, wind, and water all help to transfer pollen.

Visit me!

Flowering plants have different ways of encouraging pollination. Some have brightly colored petals and wonderful scents, but most flowers attract insects with a sweet liquid called **nectar**. As insects drink the nectar, they brush against the pollen, which sticks to their bodies and then falls off on the next flower they visit. The pollen fertilizes the flower's seeds so they can grow into new plants.

Favorite colors and perfumes

Bees tend to visit yellow, blue, and blue-green flowers. Butterflies are attracted by the scents of flowers, especially buddleia, milkweed, and verbena plants.

Yellow pollen can be seen on the tips of the stamen of these flowers.

Plants

Sunflower

poster board

colored tissue paper

foil

glue

scissors

1 Cut a circle out of poster board to make the center of your sunflower. Cut two larger circles from yellow tissue paper.

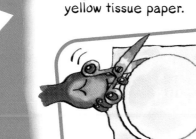

2 Place the poster board circle between the two tissue paper circles. Cut petal shapes around the edges of the tissue paper.

3 Turn the top tissue paper circle so that the petals are overlapping the ones underneath, as shown. Glue all three circles together.

PVA

4 Scrunch up colored tissue paper and silver foil into little balls. Glue these onto the center of your sunflower.

Make a bunch of sunflowers and tape sticks to the back of each, then put them in a big vase

Plant juice

Have you ever wondered how your sweater became red, or your pants blue? It is because clothes are stained using special substances called dyes. Until about 150 years ago, all dyes came from plants and animals. Today, chemical dyes are used.

Changing color

Most of the dyes we have today are made from chemicals in large factories around the world. There are now more than 3,000 different colors of dye. Before we started using chemical dyes, there were fewer than 100 natural dye colors available.

Magical blue

For over 2,000 years, blue dye was made from the woad plant. Woad was also used as a healing plant in many parts of the world. Ancient warriors in Europe colored their clothes and skin with blue dye before a battle. This not only terrified their enemies, but helped to heal their wounds as well.

Redder than red

Red dye was made from the roots of madder plants, or from dried insects that lived on the kermes oak. Turkey was one of the main countries to use the madder root to make the dye, so the vibrant color became known as Turkey red.

Plants

Tie dye T-shirt

WHAT YOU NEED

rubber bands

1 Place tea bags into a bowl or pan of hot water and leave to soak for a few hours.

2 Gather up sections of T-shirt and wind rubber bands around them, as shown.

Soak the T-shirt in the pan for a few hours. Squeeze out the excess water. Hang the T-shirt to dry.

3

tea bags

white T-shirt

Create an original design using natural dyes

4 Dip the gathered sections of T-shirt in colored ink.

inks

owl or pan

When dry, remove the rubber bands. **5**

23

Circles of time

As you grow, your arms and legs become longer and your body length increases. Each year, you become a little taller and wider. Trees grow in the same way. Their branches grow outward and become thicker and their trunks widen a little with each passing year. Like you, trees need food, water, and sunlight to keep them healthy and help them grow.

How old are you?

Trees can live for hundreds of years. Some, such as the redwood trees found in western parts of North America, are thousands of years old. You can tell how old a tree is by counting the growth rings inside the trunk. Each ring represents one year's growth.

Slow, quick, quick, slow!

Some trees have rings that are very close together. This means that weather and soil conditions were not good enough for these trees to grow very much. When the growth rings are farther apart, the trees had good growing seasons those years.

Petrified wood

Wood eventually dies and decays. In some conditions it can become **petrified wood**. This happens when water soaks into dead wood. Over time, the wood rots away and the minerals from the water harden, leaving a rock in its place. Petrified wood can look a little scary.

Petrified wood is wood that has turned into rock.

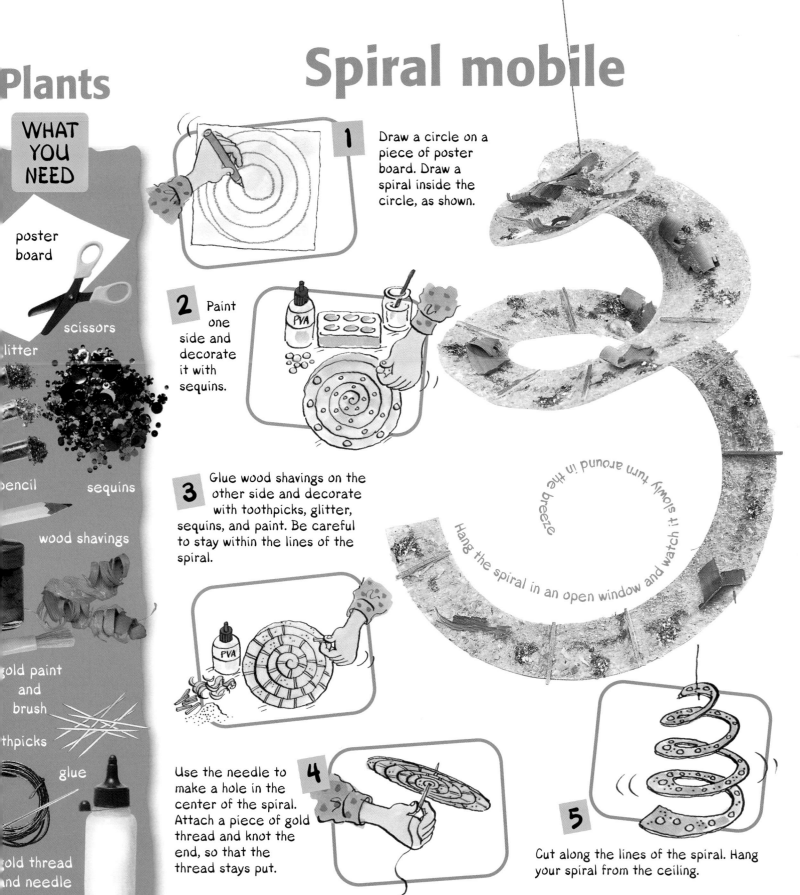

Plants

poster board

scissors

glitter

pencil

sequins

wood shavings

gold paint and brush

toothpicks

glue

gold thread and needle

Spiral mobile

1 Draw a circle on a piece of poster board. Draw a spiral inside the circle, as shown.

2 Paint one side and decorate it with sequins.

3 Glue wood shavings on the other side and decorate with toothpicks, glitter, sequins, and paint. Be careful to stay within the lines of the spiral.

4 Use the needle to make a hole in the center of the spiral. Attach a piece of gold thread and knot the end, so that the thread stays put.

5 Cut along the lines of the spiral. Hang your spiral from the ceiling.

Hang the spiral in an open window and watch it slowly turn around in the breeze

25

Fancy fossils

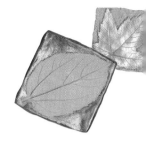

Dinosaur food

Whenever you go to an evergreen forest, you are visiting the Earth as it was millions of years ago. Evergreens are the descendants of ancient trees that were once food for early plant-eating dinosaurs. The prehistoric forests included redwood, yew, pine, cypress, and monkey puzzle trees.

Primitive plants

Horsetails and ferns were also important food for plant-eating dinosaurs. These plants grew quickly, forming enormous, swampy forests. It was not until the end of the Jurassic period, 140 million years ago, that flowering plants first appeared. They began to take over as the Earth's dominant plants, because they could spread their seeds more easily.

Strange or familiar?

If we could go back in time millions of years, we would see some strange plants as well as some that we might recognize. Cycads were early plants that looked like palm trees with woody trunks and tough leaves. Ginkgoes were tall fern-like trees that grew in high places. You can still see descendants of these plants today such as the slender, ornamental ginkgoe with fan-shaped leaves that grow along city streets.

Frozen in time

Fossils tell us what ancient plants looked like. A fossil forms when a plant or animal dies. If it falls into mud or sand, it may be preserved when the mud or sand turns into rock over millions of years.

Millions of years ago, when the first dinosaurs lived, the Earth was a very different place. Colorful, flowering plants did not yet exist. Massive forests covered much of the green landscape. Some of these ancient plant types are still around today, while others have disappeared forever. Our only images of these **extinct** species are imprinted in **fossils**.

Plants

Leaf tiles

clay

paints and brush

silver and gold paints

leaves

1 Soften the clay, then mold it into several flat, square tiles.

2 Place a leaf on a couple of tiles. Rub evenly across them. Peel off the leaves to reveal the prints. Leave to dry.

3 On another tile, use the wooden end of your paintbrush to make a leaf pattern. Leave to dry.

4 Paint your tiles.

Make a collection of different leaf patterns

27

Tree nurseries

We could not survive without trees. They breathe in harmful carbon dioxide and breathe out the oxygen humans and animals need to stay alive. Forests provide food and shelter to thousands of people, birds, animals, insects, and plants. In the past, we destroyed trees and forests without realizing the damage we were causing. Now, we are careful to grow new trees to replace the ones that are lost.

Replanting rainforests

For many years, vast areas of **rainforest** were cut down for wood, or burnt to clear land for farming. Those destroyed forests are gone forever. Today, countries have started to look after their forests. Tree nurseries have been set up so that new trees are always growing. When they are big enough, the young trees are planted in the cleared, or empty forest areas. In this way, the plants and animals that live in forest habitats are protected.

Tree houses

Animals and plants need the leafy habitats of trees to survive. Many animals, such as monkeys, birds, and bats, find food and shelter high up in the trees. Other animals, such as insects, rodents, rabbits, and snakes, make their homes underground among tree roots. Many animals also feed on the plants that grow in the forests. The soil that these plants grow in is made richer by the rotting leaves that have fallen from trees. The roots of the trees also hold the soil in place. Without trees, many other forest plants would also die.

New life

A forest that has been destroyed by fire can quickly recover. In hot, dry weather, a forest fire may burn for days, destroying thousands of acres. A few months later, new seedlings begin to sprout up from the burned and blackened ground. Slowly, the trees begin to grow and the animals, birds, insects, and plants can return to a new forest home.

Plants

Build an underground scene of a rabbit burrow

WHAT YOU NEED

large cardboard box

scissors

newspaper

paints and brush

small pebbles

rdboard

toilet paper rolls

glue

colored paper

clay

1 Cut one side out of the box and a hole in the top. Push the toilet paper roll into the hole.

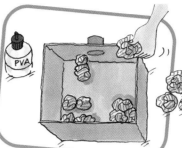

2 Glue scrunched up balls of newspaper inside the box.

3 Cut the other toilet paper roll in half. Glue the pieces between the newspaper. Leave a few empty spaces for tunnels.

4 Paint and glue pebbles inside the box. Cut a strip of grass from cardboard. Paint it and glue it onto the top of the box.

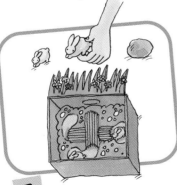

5 Mold rabbits from clay. When dry, paint them and place in the burrow.

Cut flowers and leaves from the colored paper to add to the grass.

29

Hardy plants

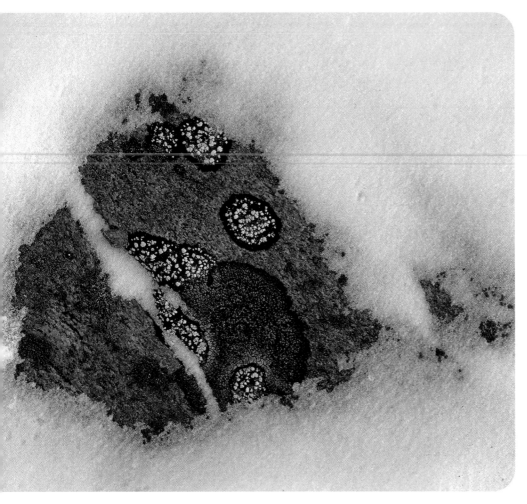

The lichen that is growing on this rock can survive in ice and snow.

In the dry, sandy desert regions of the world, the climate is very hot. On the Arctic **tundra**, the weather is so cold that the land is covered with snow and ice for most of the year. Most plants cannot survive in these extreme conditions, but there are some plants that can live in the toughest places.

On the tundra

For two or three months during the summer, the frozen tundra begins to thaw. Ice on the surface melts, but the ground below remains frozen solid. Tundra flowering plants, such as stitchwort, cranberries, and dwarf birch, spring up from the soil. Colorful lichens, mosses, **herbs**, and grasses burst into life. Most tundra plants are small and grow close to the ground to protect themselves from the wind.

Lichens

Lichens are amazing because they can live in the harshest conditions. These plants grow closer than any other plant to the North and South Poles. They provide reindeer with food during the cold Arctic months.

Water gatherers

In the desert, it rarely rains. When the rain finally does fall, it is usually a downpour. That is why succulent plants, such as **cacti** and spurge, have shallow roots that spread out a long way to quickly soak up as much water as possible. These plants also have large fleshy stems that store water for long periods of time.

Prickly plants

A long time ago, cacti had leaves instead of prickles. Leaves release moisture into the air, so very slowly, over millions of years, cacti developed prickles, or spines, to help keep moisture in.

Cactus desk organizer

WHAT YOU NEED

oilet paper rolls and
aper towel roll

newspaper

scissors

paints
and
brush

tape

ardboard
ox lid

glue

glitter

othpicks

1 Use the box lid as your base and tape the paper towel roll in one corner.

2 Glue scrunched up newspaper around the base to make different sized pockets.

3 Cut a hole in each side of the paper towel roll. Insert a toilet paper roll in each hole.

PVA

4 Glue balls of scrunched newspaper on your cactus. Then glue strips of newspaper all over and leave it to dry.

5 Paint and then decorate with glitter. Push toothpicks into the cactus to give it a spiky look.

PVA

Store pens, pencils, and paintbrushes safely in this prickly holder!

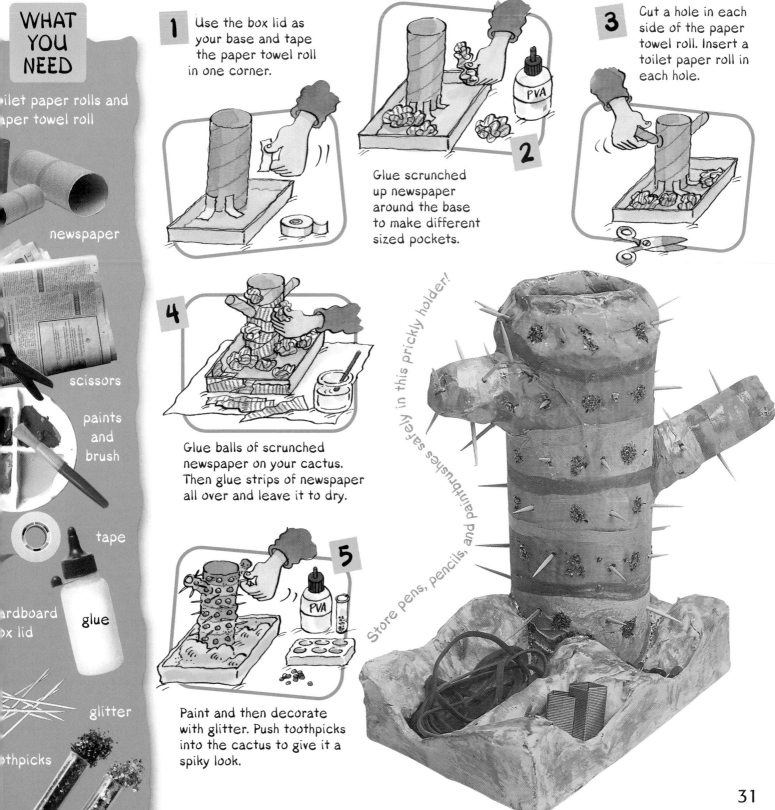

31

Vegetables

You eat many different types of plants every day. In fact, if you eat bread, you are eating grass because wheat is a type of grass. If you eat carrots, you are eating plant roots. People throughout the world eat all types of plants, from fungi to seaweed.

First farmers

Our ancestors discovered which plants and parts of plants could be eaten safely. They began to grow these plants in fields – this is known as **cultivation**. They chose the biggest and best plants from each harvest to provide seeds for the next crop. Many of today's **vegetables** are bigger and tastier than the ones our ancestors harvested.

Plant parts

The parts of plants we eat may be the roots, stems, leaves, seeds, fruits, or flowers. These parts usually have the most nutrients and are where the plants store their own supply of food. Potatoes, cassava, carrots, onions, and turnips are the swollen stems and roots of the plant. Lettuce and spinach are the leaves of their plants and cauliflower and broccoli are the flowers. Nuts and beans are the seeds. Pumpkins, squash, cucumbers, and melons are all a type of plant called **gourds**.

Different tastes

Some people do not eat meat. Instead, they live on a diet mainly of vegetables. These people are called vegetarians.

Gourd family

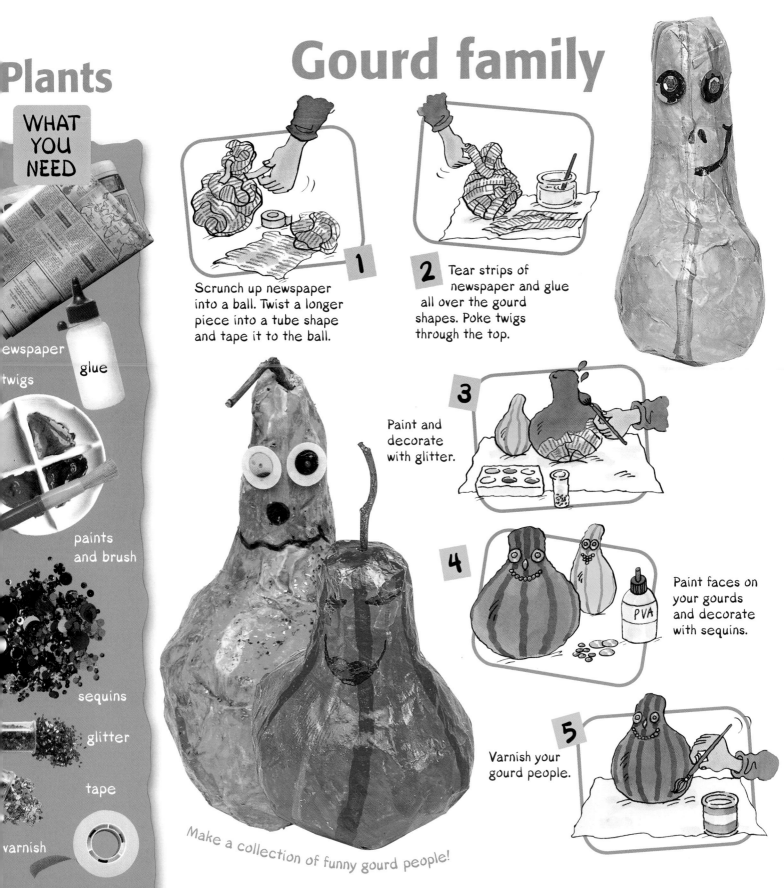

ewspaper

glue

twigs

paints
and brush

sequins

glitter

tape

varnish

1 Scrunch up newspaper into a ball. Twist a longer piece into a tube shape and tape it to the ball.

2 Tear strips of newspaper and glue all over the gourd shapes. Poke twigs through the top.

3 Paint and decorate with glitter.

4 Paint faces on your gourds and decorate with sequins.

PVA

5 Varnish your gourd people.

Make a collection of funny gourd people!

33

Paper and pulp

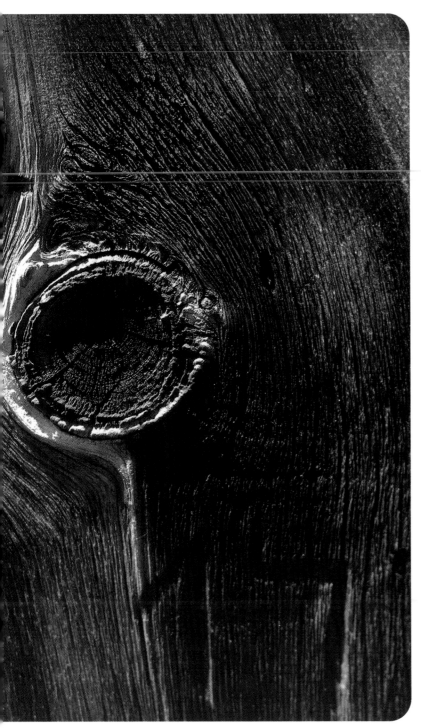

Did you know that your favorite comic book, novel, or magazine began life as a tree in a large forest far from where you live? How does a tall, leafy tree become the pages of a book?

The journey begins

The main ingredient used in paper-making is wood. Trees are cut down and taken to sawmills where the wood is cut up to make many different products. Wood chips are usually all that is left of the tree. It is these wood chips that are used to make paper.

Turn to pulp

Enormous trucks are piled high with wood chips and driven to paper mills. After the wood chips have been cleaned, they travel along a series of pipes and tubes to be made into **pulp** in large machines called refiners. Using water, steam, and large spinning discs, the wood chips become pulp.

On the wire

Pulp is mostly made of water. It is put on a fast-moving screen, called a wire, to pump the water out. Then, the pulp is pressed into sheets of paper and dried. Next, the paper is ironed or smoothed and wound into a giant roll. The paper is later cut to different sizes.

Delivery time

Once the paper is cut, trucks or trains take it to destinations all over the world. The paper is now ready to become your favorite book or comic.

Plants

Handmade paper

WHAT YOU NEED

dishcloth

bowl

paints

glitter

ewspaper

wire mesh

grass and leaves

1 Tear some newspaper into small pieces and place in a large bowl of water. Leave it to soak overnight.

2 Drain and transfer the newspaper pulp to another bowl. Add paint for color.

3 Slide the wire mesh under the pulp and lift it out. Place on top of newspaper.

4 Press down hard all over with a dishcloth to flatten the pulp.

Flip the pulp over. Remove the wire mesh and leave to dry.

5

You can make a collage from your homemade paper

Adding glitter, leaves, or other items to the pulp will give your paper an interesting texture.

35

Dropping leaves

Have you ever wondered why leaves change color? Some trees that grow in cold winter climates lose their leaves in order to survive the freezing weather. Before dropping from the trees, the leaves turn yellow, orange, or red because water stops reaching them. The leaves slowly die, fall to the ground, and turn brown.

Autumn leaves

Trees that shed their leaves in winter are called deciduous trees. They grow in parts of the world where the climate is **temperate**, such as North America, southern Europe, and Asia.

Oak, maple, ash, birch, and beech are all deciduous trees that lose their leaves. In the middle of winter, their branches are bare. Then, in the early spring, these trees burst into life as new buds and blossoms appear. As the weather warms, leaves and fruits start to grow on their branches once again.

Evergreens

Some trees do not change color in autumn, or drop their leaves during winter. These trees are known as evergreens and include fir, spruce, pine, and cypress trees. They are very tough plants that hold onto the water stored inside them. When winter comes and water in the ground turns to ice, they still have a store of water to live on.

No seasons

In the tropical rainforests that grow in regions near the equator, weather conditions are sunny, warm, and wet, so trees grow all year. Most of these trees are evergreens, but there are some deciduous trees as well. Deciduous trees that grow here do not drop their leaves all at once. They replace them, one by one, as they drop off.

Plants

Four seasons collage

Give each tree a seasonal look

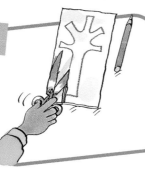

1 Draw an outline of a tree trunk and branches on the poster board and cut it out.

Trace the outline of your tree onto four separate pieces of paper.

2

3 Cut strips of textured paper and glue them onto the trunks.

4 Paint the backgrounds. Cut leaf shapes from the tissue paper and glue onto your trees.

Spring

Summer

Autumn

Winter

Cotton ball blossoms

Wind wire around a twig. Tear off small pieces of cotton balls and tissue paper. Wrap the ends of the wires around them. Now decorate your cotton ball blossoms with glitter.

37

Exploding spores

If you stroll through a dark forest or anywhere it is damp, you will find mosses, ferns, lichens, and liverworts. They are all ancient plant types. In fact, many of these plants were around millions of years ago, at the time of the dinosaurs. They are known as non-flowering plants because they do not have flowers and they make spores instead of seeds.

Velvety moss

In damp sunless places you can see carpets of green moss growing. If you were to take a good look at a piece of moss, you would see many slender stems covered with small green leaves. Underneath the leaves are tiny hairs that attach themselves to the ground. On the stalks above the leaves are teardrop-shaped capsules containing tiny spores. The capsules burst and the spores are carried away by the wind. New mosses grow where they land.

Feathery ferns

Thousands of years ago, plant-eating dinosaurs munched on ferns. Many ferns have feather-like leaves, or fronds, that are divided into little leaflets. Ferns form spores on the underside of their leaves. The stems of most ferns grow underground.

Liverworts and lichens

Liverworts produce spores that develop inside little capsules. Lichens also produce spores. Lichens are actually two plants living together – a fungus and an **alga**. The alga supplies the fungus with food. The fungus protects the alga and supplies it with water.

When a moss capsule explodes, it releases a cloud of spores.

Fern forest

2 Paint one side of some ferns dark green and blue, and others violet and black.

1 Paint a pale green and yellow background on white poster board.

3 Put the green and blue painted ferns face down on the painted poster board. Place a piece of paper over the leaves. Gently rub over the leaves with your hand.

4 Remove the paper to reveal the prints. Now lay the violet and black-painted ferns over the top. Repeat the printing exercise for a shadowy forest effect.

Use ferns to print decorative borders on your personal mail

You can make a snowy scene by printing white and gold ferns on black poster board.

39

Wings and pods

It is not just humans that use helicopters and parachutes to move around. So do seeds! Plants use all sorts of weird ways to spread their seeds – watch out for firecrackers, catapults, and explosions!

Silky parachutes

One dandelion plant produces hundreds of seeds. When the weather is dry, the seed head opens to reveal delicate silky parachutes, each one containing a seed. A gentle breeze is enough to carry the parachutes far away.

Helicopter wings

Sycamore and maple trees have seeds inside winged cases that look like helicopter blades. This allows the seeds to travel long distances through the air.

Take aim and... fire!

Vetches belong to the pea-family of plants. These plants have catapults to launch their seeds into the air. As the sun dries out the case that contains their seeds, it stretches tight. Eventually the case splits open, firing the plant's seeds into the air, like a catapult.

Exploding fruit

Sometimes the fruits of a plant explode, spreading the seeds inside through the air. The seed pods of beans dry out and explode like firecrackers, flinging their seeds a long way away.

Hitching a ride

Burr and cleaver fruits have tiny hooks that can become attached to an animal's fur. Unknowingly, the animals carry these plants from place to place, dropping seeds as they go.

A dandelion seed head.

Pine cone parachute

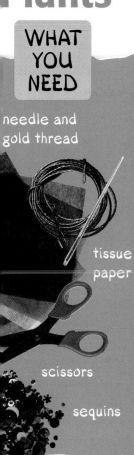

needle and gold thread

tissue paper

scissors

sequins

white plastic bag
(check with an adult first, as plastic bags can be dangerous)

glue

pine cone

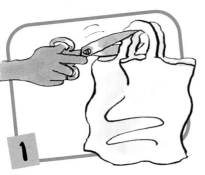

1 Cut the handles off the white plastic bag.

2 Decorate the bag with colored tissue paper, sequins, and paint.

3 Use the needle to poke four holes through the edges of the bag. Thread four equal pieces of thread through the holes, knotting the ends.

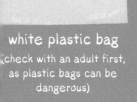

4 Tie a pine cone to the other ends of the threads.

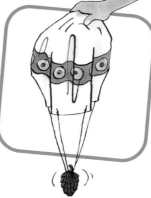

Take your parachute outside and let the wind carry it away

41

Medicinal plants

What would you think if your doctor gave you peppermint for your headache, or ginger if you felt sick? Long ago, that is what would have happened. Healers gave plants to people to make them feel better. These plants became known as medicinal plants, many of which are still used as **medicine** today.

Then and now

Long ago, plants used as medicine, such as lavender and ginseng, were grown in special gardens. People known as herbalists wrote about the healing qualities of these plants in books called herbals. Today, science and nature work together. Many modern medicines contain natural plant ingredients as well as ingredients made by people. Scientists journey through forests all over the world, examining plants in search of new cures.

Essential oils

Ancient herbalists used plant **oils** to heal wounds and infections. The oils were taken from the flowers, fruits, bark, and roots of plants and trees. Today, oils taken from the aloe vera and jojoba plants are still used to soothe skin problems.

Healing power

Some North American Native peoples used the bark and leaves of the witch hazel plant to heal injuries, such as cuts and swelling. They also used parts of the white willow tree to relieve pain. Hundreds of years later, modern scientists used the leaves and bark of the white willow tree to make the very first form of aspirin.

Purple lavender has been used as a healing plant.

Plants

WHAT YOU NEED

erbs and spices

aintbrush

wigs

black or gray
poster board

glue

old paint

1 Glue twigs on the poster board to make tree trunks and branches.

2 Use different kinds of spices to create a variety of leaves for the trees. Glue them in place.

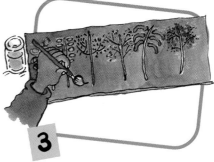

3 When dry, add gold paint to the background for a highlighting effect.

Create a scented forest scene that shimmers and shines

Amazing plants

Sundews, flytraps, and pitchers may not sound like varieties of plants, but they are! Most plants get the nutrients they need from soil and water, but others cannot. Plants that grow in places where the soil is poor have had to find unusual ways of catching the food they need.

It's a trap!

A Venus flytrap sets a trap for unsuspecting insects and when it catches them, it eats them! Venus flytraps have large, hinged leaves with spiky teeth. These leaves stay open to attract insects to the plant's nectar. When an insect lands on one of the leaves, the two halves snap shut, trapping the insect inside. The plant then slowly **digests** its meal.

Meat eaters

Pitcher plants are shaped like large deep vases. Insects are attracted by the sweet-smelling nectar produced in the rim of the leaf. When an insect lands on the edge of the leaf, it slips and falls into a deep pool of liquid. There it is digested by the plant. Other meat eaters, such as butterwort and sundew plants, attract insects to their sticky leaves. Once an insect lands on the sticky surface, it cannot get away.

Big old stinky!

The world's heaviest flower is a species of rafflesia that grows on the roots of vines in tropical rainforest of Southeast Asia. It is so big that a child could sit on it. You would not want to, though, because it smells like rotting meat!

A fly is caught in the deadly leaves of a Venus flytrap.

Giant rafflesia

Plants

WHAT YOU NEED

- small cardboard box
- paints and brush
- tissue paper
- sequins
- glue
- newspaper and scissors
- pencil
- tape
- glitter

1 Draw a circle on the box. Wrap strips of newspaper around the edge of the circle. Tape into place.

2 Glue strips of newspaper all over the box.

3 Paint and decorate with glitter.

4 Draw five or six petals on tissue paper, as shown. Cut them out. Glue on sequins and glitter.

5 Now glue the petals on top of the box.

Use your rafflesia as a container for potted plants

Glossary

alga A simple plant that grows in water, such as seaweed.

amber Hardened brown fluid, called resin, from an ancient tree.

bonsai A miniature tree developed in Japan.

cambium The inner layer of bark from which new wood and bark grow.

carbon dioxide The gas taken in by plants. It is harmful to humans.

cells The smallest part of a living thing. Cells can grow, feed, and reproduce.

cereal A grass, the seeds of which are used for food. Wheat, rice, barley, maize, and oats are all cereals.

chlorophyll Green pigment, or coloring, that plants use to make food from sunlight.

chloroplasts The tiny parts of a green plant that contain chlorophyll.

cultivation Caring for the land in order to grow plants for food.

deciduous Plants that drop their leaves during cold winters.

digest To break down food into a form than can be used by the body.

edible Food that is safe to eat.

evergreens Plants that keep their leaves all year.

extinct No longer in existence.

fertilize To combine the male cell with the female cell to form a seed.

fertilizer A substance that is added to soil to help plants grow.

fossil The remains of a living thing, preserved in rock.

fungi Simple plants that do not contain chlorophyll. Mushrooms and toadstools are fungi.

germinate To grow from a seed or spore.

gourds Pumpkins, melons, and cucumbers are gourds.

habitat The surroundings in which a plant lives.

herbs Aromatic plants used in cooking and medicine. Peppermint and dandelions are herbs.

latex The white milky liquid of the rubber tree which is tapped to make rubber.

lenticels The breathing holes in the surface of tree bark.

medicine A substance used to treat illness. Some plants, such as lavender and ginseng, are used to make medicine.

minerals Natural substances, such as iron, needed by plants.

nectar A sweet liquid made by flowers to attract insects to them.

nutrients The good things found in food that help animals and plants live and grow.

oil A greasy liquid taken from plants that can be used in medicine and cooking. Aloe vera and jojoba plants provide healing oils.

organic Something that comes from living things.

oxygen The essential gas given off by all plants.

paddies Flooded fields where rice is grown, especially in Asia.

petrified wood Ancient trees in which minerals from water inside the trees have turned to stone.

photosynthesis The process by which plants use sunlight to turn water and carbon dioxide into food.

pigment A substance that gives color to plants or animals.

plantation An area where trees or crops have been planted for harvesting.

pollen A powder made by a plant's stamen containing the male cells.

pollinating Transfering pollen from the male part of one flower to the female part of another.

pulp Watery ground-up wood.

rainforest A thick evergreen forest, with heavy rainfall all year.

resin A substance that oozes out of the bark of a tree to protect a wound.

spice Any aromatic plant used in cooking

spores Tiny cells produced by ferns, mosses, and fungi that grow into a new plant.

stamen The male part of a flower.

starch The food created and stored in the parts of a plant.

stigma The tip of the female part of a flower.

stomata Tiny holes on the underside of a leaf.

temperate A mild climate, between the hot tropics and cold poles.

tundra A large snow-covered area of land on the edge of the Arctic where trees do not grow.

Index

algae 38, 46
amber 8, 46

bark 8-9, 16, 18, 42, 46
barley 10
bees 16, 20
blossom 36
bonsai trees 14, 46
branches 14, 24, 36
butterflies 20

cacti 30-31, 46
cambium 8, 46
carbon dioxide 4, 8, 12, 28, 46
cells 4, 8, 46
cereal 10, 32, 46
chemical 10, 18, 22
chlorophyll 4, 6, 46
chloroplast 4
cinnamon 8
climate 26, 30
cork 8
crops 10, 32, 46
cultivation 32, 46
cycads 26

deciduous 4, 36, 46
deserts 30
dinasours 26, 38
dwarf trees 14
dyes 22-23, 46

evergreen trees 4, 14, 26, 36, 46

fairy rings 6
fan orchids 17
farming 10, 28, 32
fern forest painting 38
fertilize 10, 14, 20
flower 12, 16, 20, 26, 32, 38, 42
forests 16, 26, 28-29, 34, 36
fossils 8, 26, 46
fruits 12, 32, 40, 42, 46
fungi 6, 16, 32, 38, 46

germinate 12, 46
gourds 32, 33, 46

grasses 10, 30, 32
growth rings 24

habitat 14, 28
herbs 30, 40, 42, 46

latex 18, 46
leaves 4, 8, 12, 26, 28, 30, 32, 36, 38, 42, 44
lenticels 8, 46
lichens 30, 38
liverworts 38

madder plant 22
maize 10
medicine 42, 46
minerals 12, 24, 46
mosses 30, 38
mushrooms 6-7

nectar 20, 44, 46
nutrients 6, 10, 12, 44, 46

oils 42, 46
orchids 16-17
organic 16, 46
oxygen 8, 28, 46

paddies 10, 46
petals 20
petrified wood 24, 46
photosynthesis 4, 46
pigment 6, 46
plantations 18, 46
pollen 16, 20, 46
pollination 16, 46

prehistoric forests 26
pulp 34, 46

rainforests 16, 28, 36, 46
resin 8, 46
rice 10-11, 32
rings in trees 24, 46
roots 4, 12, 14, 28, 30, 32, 42
rubber trees 18-19

sap 18, 46
scents 16, 20
seasons 4, 12, 30, 36-37
seeds 6, 10, 12, 16, 20, 28, 32, 38, 40, 46
soil 10, 12, 24, 28, 44, 46
spices 8, 46
spores 6, 38, 46
stamen 20, 46
starch 4, 46
stems 4, 30, 32, 38
stigma 20
stomata 4, 46
sugars 4
sunlight 4, 12, 24

temperate 36, 46
toadstool 6
trees 4, 8, 12, 14, 16, 18, 24, 26, 28, 34, 38 40, 42
tropical rainforest plants 16, 36

trunks 8, 14, 16, 18, 24, 34
tundra 30, 46

vegetables 32, 46
Venus flytraps 44

water 4, 12, 20, 24, 30, 34, 36, 38, 44
weather 24, 28, 30
wheat 10, 32
woad plant 22

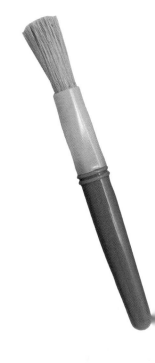

Materials guide

A list of materials, how to use them, and suitable alternatives

The crafts in this book require the use of materials and products that are easily purchased in craft stores. If you cannot locate some materials, you can substitute other materials with those we have listed here, or use your imagination to make the craft with what you have on hand.

Gold foil: can be found in craft stores. It is very delicate and sometimes tears.

Silver foil: can be found in craft stores. It is very delicate, soft and sometimes tears. For some crafts, tin or aluminum foil can be substituted. Aluminum foil is a less delicate material and makes a harder finished craft.

PVA glue: commonly called polyvinyl acetate. It is a modeling glue that creates a type of varnish when mixed with water. It is also used as a strong glue. In some crafts, other strong glues can be substituted, and used as an adhesive, but not as a varnish.

Filler paste: sometimes called plaster of Paris. It is a paste that hardens when it dries. It can be purchased at craft and hardware stores.

Paste: a paste of 1/2 cup flour, one tablespoon of salt and one cup of warm water can be made to paste strips of newspaper as in a papier mâché craft. Alternatively, wallpaper paste can be purchased and mixed as per directions on the package.

Cellophane: a clear or colored plastic material. Acetate can also be used in crafts that call for this material. Acetate is a clear, or colored, thin plastic that can be found in craft stores.

gold foil

silver foil

filler paste

PVA glue

flour

salt

cellophane or acetate

2 3 4 5 6 7 8 9 0   Printed in the USA 0 9 8 7 6 5 4

Written by Megan Faulkner
Designed by Kat Peruyera
Cover and package designed by Bill Henderson

Copyright© 2015 Scholastic Inc.

tangerine
Press
an imprint of
■SCHOLASTIC
www.scholastic.com

Scholastic and Tangerine Press and associated logos are trademarks of Scholastic Inc.

Published by Tangerine Press, an imprint of Scholastic Inc.; 557 Broadway, New York, NY 10012

10 9 8 7 6 5 4 3 2 1

ISBN 978-0-545-85148-0

Printed and bound in Guangzhou, China

Photos ©: box paper scrap: t_kimura/iStockphoto; box water: ddbell/iStockphoto; box shark fins: SSSCCC/iStockphoto; box sharks: ap-images/iStockphoto; cover main: Mike Parry/Getty Images; back cover water: Maks Narodenko/Shutterstock, Inc.; 1 background: Andrey_Kuzmin/Shutterstock, Inc.; 2 main: Jim Abernethy/Getty Images; 3 top: www.Narchuk.com/Getty Images; 3 top paper: SCOTTCHAN/Shutterstock, Inc.; 3 center top: Creation/Shutterstock, Inc.; 3 center bottom: Jim Abernethy/Getty Images; 3 bottom: Chris Ross/Getty Images; 3 background: Jim Abernethy/Getty Images; 4 background: CoreyFord/iStockphoto; 4 bottom left: STILLFX/Shutterstock, Inc.; 4 bottom right: STILLFX/iStockphoto; 5 center: Catmando/Shutterstock, Inc.; 5 bottom teeth: Masterfile; 5 bottom left: donatas1205/Shutterstock, Inc.; 5 background: CoreyFord/iStockphoto; 6 background: Chris Ross/Getty Images; 6 bottom: moyogo/Wikimedia; 6 center left: Josh Humbert/Getty Images; 7 top: etraveler/iStockphoto; 7 bottom: bonishphotography/iStockphoto; 7 paper scrap: xpixel/Shutterstock, Inc.; 7 background: Chris Ross/Getty Images; 7 center: Hilton Mantooth; 8 main: Ruth Petzold/Getty Images; 9 top: David Jenkins/Robert Harding World Imagery/Corbis Images; 9 background: Ruth Petzold/Getty Images; 10 main: Education Images/UIG; 11 bottom right: STILLFX/Shutterstock, Inc.; 11 bottom left: NaluPhoto/iStockphoto; 11 background: Education Images/UIG; 12 main: Education Images/UIG/Getty Images; 13 center left: Greg Amptman/Shutterstock, Inc.; 13 center left photo frames: rangizzz/Shutterstock, Inc.; 13 center right: STILLFX/Shutterstock, Inc.; 13 bottom left: Matt9122/Shutterstock, Inc.; 13 bottom right: Devonyu/iStockphoto; 13 background: Education Images/UIG/Getty Images; 14 main: Karen Doody/Stocktrek Images/Getty Images; 15 center: MP cz/Shutterstock, Inc.; 15 bottom: ZWEID/iStockphoto; 15 main: Karen Doody/Stocktrek Images/Getty Images; 15 bottom photo frame: SCOTTCHAN/Shutterstock, Inc.; 16 main: stephaniki2/iStockphoto; 17 top: qldian/iStockphoto; 17 center: qldian/iStockphoto; 17 bottom: CAlleaume/iStockphoto; 17 background: stephaniki2/iStockphoto; 17 photo frames: SCOTTCHAN/Shutterstock, Inc.; 18 main: Matt9122/Shutterstock, Inc.; 19 center left: Shane Gross/Shutterstock, Inc.; 19 bottom left: ilbusca/iStockphoto; 19 bottom right: Matt9122/Shutterstock, Inc.; 19 background: Matt9122/Shutterstock, Inc.; 19 photo frame: SCOTTCHAN/Shutterstock, Inc.; 20 main: stephaniki2/iStockphoto; 21 top: UWphotographer/iStockphoto; 21 bottom right: JudiLen/iStockphoto; 21 bottom left: ShaneGross/iStockphoto; 21 background: stephaniki2/iStockphoto; 21 photo frames: SCOTTCHAN/Shutterstock, Inc.; 22 main: Alexander Sofonov/Barcroft Media/Getty Images; 23 center: Tui De Roy/Getty Images; 23 bottom: kamonchanok5211224102/iStockphoto; 23 background: Alexander Sofonov/Barcroft Media/Getty Images; 23 photo frame: SCOTTCHAN/Shutterstock, Inc.; 24 background: BryanToro/iStockphoto; 24 bottom: bonishphotography/iStockphoto; 24 photo frame: SCOTTCHAN/Shutterstock, Inc.; 25 center: Brian J. Skerry/Getty Images; 25 bottom: Mark Conlin/Getty Images; 25 background: BryanToro/iStockphoto; 25 photo frame: SCOTTCHAN/Shutterstock, Inc.; 26 main: Jim Abernethy/Getty Images; 27 bottom: NaluPhoto/iStockphoto; 27 background: Jim Abernethy/Getty Images; 27 photo frame: SCOTTCHAN/Shutterstock, Inc.; 28 background: dioch/Shutterstock, Inc.; 28 top: Entienou/iStockphoto; 28 center left: Stephen Frink/Getty Images; 28 center right: Steven Trainoff Ph.D./Getty Images; 29 top: atese/iStockphoto; 29 bottom: BlueRingMedia/Shutterstock, Inc.; 29 background: dioch/Shutterstock, Inc.; 30 background: Willyam Bradberry/Shutterstock, Inc.; 31 top: david olah/iStockphoto; 31 center top: bgton/iStockphoto; 31 center bottom: Fox Photos/Getty Images; 31 bottom left: Raphael Christinat/Shutterstock, Inc.; 31 bottom right: Anastasios71/Shutterstock, Inc.; 31 background: Willyam Bradberry/Shutterstock, Inc.; 31 photo frame: SCOTTCHAN/Shutterstock, Inc.; 32 background: Swimwitdafishes/iStockphoto; 32 paper scrap: xpixel/Shutterstock, Inc.

Attack and fatality statistics are from the International Shark Attack File (ISAF), Florida Museum of Natural History, University of Florida. All statistics are for unprovoked attacks.

SHARK!

The word alone makes pulses race and eyes widen with fear. Images of massive mouths bearing down with razor-sharp, flesh-ripping teeth are imprinted on our minds. Though more humans are killed each year by vending machines—sharks, above any land predator—continue to be a source of terror and fascination.

Think You Know Sharks?

Though sharks have cruised the planet for 400 million years, we still have a lot to learn about these mysterious creatures. Sharks are challenging to study in the field because they are elusive, dangerous, and prone to migrating across enormous watery distances. Capturing specimens for observation isn't an option because most sharks die very quickly in captivity.

We still have so many unanswered questions about sharks! On the positive side, scientists are sharing fascinating new discoveries about sharks every day. Our journey toward understanding these amazing beasts is just beginning!

MEGAL

Although a face-to-face encounter with a hungry great white is most people's worst nightmare, modern apex predators are mere whispers of their forefish.

During the 14th to 17th century, gigantic triangular fossils as large as a man's hand were found embedded in rock. Believed to be the petrified tongues of dragons and snakes, these "tongue stones" were thought to be an antidote for poisons and toxins. Noblemen and royalty wore them as pendants or kept them in their pockets as good-luck charms. These were not dragon teeth. They were shark teeth belonging to Megalodon—perhaps the most fearsome predator to ever exist on Earth.

In its day, Megalodon cruised the oceans eating giant sea turtles like potato chips and attacking whales as if they were chew toys.

Rumors persist that Megalodon isn't extinct but is secretly trolling the depths of our oceans. Although it's thrilling to imagine such a beast is still out there, scientific facts prove otherwise. When the water temperature changed and their food sources died out, so too did Megalodon.

ODON
(Carcharodon megalodon)

Lived:
15.9 million–2.6 million years ago during the Cenozoic Era (middle Miocene to end of Pliocene)

Claim to Fame:
Largest marine predator EVER

Size:
Length: Estimates range from 52–80 ft (16–24 m)
Weight: Estimates range from 53–114 tons (48–103 metric tons)

Distinguishing Characteristics:
A huge, stocky body with a giant mouth full of enormous teeth. Picture a mouth with fins.

Habitat:
Megalodon is believed to have hunted all the oceans in a wide range of marine environments–no region was spared its voracious appetite!

Diet:
Whales, dolphins, sea turtles, land creatures taking a dip

Hunting Style:
1. Open mouth
2. Swallow prey

Natural Predators:
NONE

A shark loses and replaces around 35,000 teeth over its lifespan.

Without a skeleton, scientists can only make educated guesses about Megalodon's size based on the similarity of the fossilized teeth to those of today's great white. Reaching lengths more than 7 in (17.78 cm), Megalodon teeth are the same shape and have the same serrated edges as the great white. Scientists have differing theories about Megalodon's size. At this point, we just don't know which one is correct.

Because shark skeletons are made of cartilage (the flexible connective tissue that makes your ears bendy), and cartilage breaks down over time, all that remains of prehistoric sharks are their teeth.

5

THE DANGER ZONE

Most unprovoked shark attacks happen off the Atlantic coast of Florida in the United States. Australia has the second highest number of attacks, followed by South Africa. These rankings are not concrete, however, because attacks in South Africa are not documented as they are elsewhere. Despite having the highest number of recorded attacks, only about 16 attacks occur per year in the United States, and one fatality every two years.

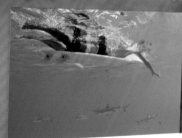

Map of World's Unprovoked Shark Attacks 1580–2014:

- 500 or more
- 200-499
- 40-199
- 1-39

Last updated Feb 20, 2014, International Shark Attack File, Florida Museum of Natural History, University of Florida

Though movies such as *Jaws* and shows from *Shark Week* make it look like sharks are hungry for human blood, the truth is we don't have the fat-to-bone ratio that a shark looks for in a tasty snack. Most shark attacks on humans are a case of mistaken identity. Unfortunately, such powerful jaws and sharp teeth mean a tiny taste test can result in fatal or disfiguring bites to a human body.

CAUTION!

SHARKS!

Human-Shark encounters usually fall into one of three categories:

The "Hit and Run" Attack: The most common type of encounter; the shark mistakes a human for prey and takes a bite, realizes its mistake, then releases and retreats. Often the victim does not even see the shark.

The "Bump and Bite" Attack: The shark circles the victim and gives it an exploratory bump, then moves in for multiple strikes. These are often severe wounds resulting in death. The motive is likely feeding or antagonistic behavior rather than mistaken identity.

The "Sneak" Attack: A series of vicious strikes with no warning bump.

Profile of the average shark victim

The longer you spend in shark-infested waters, the higher your chance of being attacked. For this reason, males between the ages of 18 and 35 who spend a lot of time surfing and swimming along the coast of Florida are the most likely to have an encounter with a shark.

A Shark Attack Story

Hilton Mantooth, a 16-year-old surfer, was never really concerned about being bitten by a shark, even though he was swimming in shark-infested waters. "Sure, I've seen them out there. I've even been chased, but my friends and I didn't really think about it," he said. On one fateful day, Hilton and his friends were surfing the inlet at New Smyrna Beach, Fla. He was sitting on his board with his feet dangling in the water when what he thinks was a blacktip shark attacked him from underneath. The shark bit his foot twice before deciding that he wasn't a meal. Hilton says, "I'll definitely get back in the water as soon as I can. The shark was just doing what animals do— feeding. They need to be respected. After all, I was in their home."

GREAT WHITE SHARK

(Carcharodon carcharias)

As the most famous, most feared, and most awe-inspiring of the shark family, the great white needs little introduction. To say it is top of the food chain is an understatement. The largest predatory fish on the planet is a lean, mean killing machine. Averaging 15 ft (5 m) in length and reaching speeds up to 35 mph (50 kmh), the great white's equally impressive brain coordinates brute force with sensory information to take down its prey of choice. New research shows the great white is more social than was believed. Complex relationships exist between sharks that humans are only beginning to understand.

Great whites may be the most frightening shark, but they are not the largest. That honor goes to the whale shark (*Rhincodon typus*), which averages 45 ft (14 m) in length and weighs around 47,000 lbs (21.5 mt). That's one BIG fish!

With a single bite, a great white can take in up to 31 lbs. (14 kg) of flesh!

Claim to Fame:
Biggest threat to humans

Size:
Average length: 13-17 ft (4-5 m)
Average weight: 4,000-7,000 lbs (680-1,100 kg)

Body Count:
Total attacks: 279
Fatal attacks: 78

Distinguishing Characteristics:
Great whites have a gray to gray-brown upper body and white belly. They have large, serrated, triangular teeth.

Habitat:
Worldwide in temperate and subtropical oceans, with a preference for cooler waters. Inshore waters around rocky reefs and islands, and often near seal colonies.

Diet:
Marine mammals, fish, sea birds

Hunting Style:
The "spy-hopping" technique involves lifting its head above the water to look for prey. Approaching its prey from below at speeds up to 35 mph (50 km) per hour, the great white partially or completely clears the water, a behavior known as breaching. Disabling its prey with the first powerful bite, the great white retreats until the victim is weakened from blood loss, then returns to devour the remains.

Natural Predators:
Orca

Lifespan:
70+ years

BULL SHARK.

(Carcharhinus leucas)

hough great whites are #1 in terms of human attacks, the bull shark is at least as much of a threat to humans. Aside from their brute strength and awesome bite power, bulls can cross from saltwater to freshwater with ease. This sneaky ability gives them access to freshwater rivers and estuaries where humans aren't expecting them, contributing to

Claim to Fame:
Freshwater/saltwater switch hitter

Size:
Average length:
7.5 ft (2.2 m)
Average weight:
209–290 lbs (95–130 kg)

Body Count
Total attacks: 93
Fatal attacks: 67

Distinguishing Characteristics:
"Bull" comes from their stocky shape, blunt snout, small eyes, and aggressive, unpredictable behavior.

Habitat:
Worldwide in the warm shallow waters around coasts and rivers, freshwater estuaries and rivers, and brackish shallows.

Diet:
Bony fish and other sharks (including other bull sharks), turtles, birds, dolphins, terrestrial mammals, crustaceans, and stingrays

Hunting Style:
Bulls are primarily solo hunters. They prefer to attack in murky water so their prey cannot see them coming. The "bump-and-bite" method is often used.

Natural Predators:
Tiger sharks, great whites, larger bull sharks, saltwater crocodiles

Lifespan:
12–16 years

the 2..1-02 .ason.

Bull sharks will throw up their stomach contents to distract predators. As the predator moves in to eat the regurgitated food, the bull shark has an opportunity to escape.

11

TIGER SHARK

(Galeocerdo cuvier)

The tiger shark is known for the variety of its diet. Some sharks are picky eaters, focusing their efforts on seals and other favorites, but not the tiger shark. Plump sea bird or tin can, juicy squid or suit of armor—it's all in a day's lunch for a tiger shark! In addition to being a voracious eater, the tiger shark prowls a broad range of habitats—shallow reefs, harbors, and canals—increasing the potential for human encounters.

Claim to Fame:
Garbage can of the sea

Size:
Average length: 12 ft (4 m)
Average weight: 849–1,400 lbs (385–635 kg)

Body Count:
Total attacks: 101
Fatal attacks: 28

Distinguishing Characteristics:
Dark black spots and vertical stripes down the body.

Habitat:
Worldwide in temperate and tropical waters, with the exception of the Mediterranean Sea. Murky waters in coastal areas and open oceans.

Diet:
Crustaceans, marine mammals, fish, jellyfish, squid, turtles, sea snakes, smaller sharks, various inedible man-made items

Hunting Style:
The tiger shark circles its prey and investigates by prodding it with its snout. When attacking, the shark often eats its prey whole, although larger prey is eaten in large bites and finished over time.

Natural Predators:
Larger tiger sharks

Lifespan:
12+ years

Weird Diet

The following items have been found inside the stomachs of tiger sharks:
A polar bear, reindeer, musical instruments, license plates, tires, a chicken coop with chickens, suit of armor, fur coat, barrel of nails, driver's license, porcupine, dogs (some wearing collars), video camera, horse head, bag of money, pigs, sheep, Barbie doll, tools, bottles of wine, 16th-century medallion, cannonball and other live munitions, bag of potatoes, jewelry, pair of pants, empty wallet, hyenas, monkeys, boat cushions, unopened can of salmon, cats, can of peas, human parts.

SAND TIGER SHARK

(Carcharias Taurus)

With its wide mouth and haphazard teeth, the sand tiger is known for its deceptively fearsome looks and docile personality. Reluctant to engage with humans unless provoked, the sand tiger is one of the few species of shark able to survive in captivity. Its laid-back personality, menacing appearance, and ability to thrive in captivity makes it the most likely species to be seen in an aquarium.

Claim to Fame:
Shark most in need of orthodontics

Size:
Average length:
6.5–10 ft (2–3 m)
Average weight:
200–350 lbs (90–160 kg)

Body Count:
Total attacks: 29
Fatal attacks: 2

Distinguishing Characteristics:
The sand tiger has a gray-brown back and pale underside. Adults have reddish-brown spots. Long, narrow, sharp teeth impale fish.

Habitat:
Sandy coastal waters, estuaries, shallow bays, and rocky or tropical reefs

Diet:
Small bony fish, rays, skates, squid, crustaceans, smaller sharks

Hunting Style:
Taking a gulp of air at the surface and holding it in its stomach to stay buoyant, the virtually motionless sand tiger silently glides up beside its prey, then attacks with a quick sideways snap. Yikes!

Natural Predators:
Larger sand tiger sharks

Lifespan:
15+ years

A sand tiger shark in captivity

15

BLACKTIP SHARK

(Carcharhinus limbatus)

ast and energetic, the nimble blacktip is known for leaping above the water and performing multiple spins in the air in pursuit of prey. These spins are the spectacular finale of a feeding run. The shark corkscrews through a school of fish grabbing as many fish as it can at a very high speed. The momentum created propels the shark completely

Claim to Fame:
Most acrobatic

Size:
Average length:
5–9 ft (1.5–2.7 m)
Average weight:
66–220 lbs (30–100 kg)

Body Count:
Total attacks: 28
Fatal attacks: 1

Distinguishing Characteristics:
Named for its black-trimmed fins, the blacktip has a long, pointy snout and distinct white band along its flank.

Habitat:
Coastal and subtropical waters around the world including brackish waters. Waters less than 100 ft deep (30 m), muddy bays, island lagoons, and drop-offs near coral reefs, mangrove swamps

Diet:
Small schooling fish, boney fish, rays and skates, smaller sharks, crustaceans, and the odd cephalopod

Hunting Style:
Blacktips are social and live and hunt in groups. Timid by nature, they become aggressive and competitive around prey resulting in a feeding frenzy.

Natural Predators:
Larger sharks

Lifespan:
12+ years

The blacktip performs a weird dance when threatened. It swims toward the threat then turns away, all the while rolling from side to side, lowering its pectoral fins, tilting its head and tail upward, and making sideways biting motions. (Try this next time you go swimming.)

GREAT HAMMER-HEAD

(Sphyrna mokarran)

Of the nine species of hammerhead sharks, the great hammerhead is the largest. Its unique hammer-shaped head (called a *cephalofoil*) makes it the easiest shark to identify. A solo hunter by night, by day the hammerhead gathers in schools 100-strong.

Claim To Fame:
Weirdest-looking head

Size:
Average length:
13–20 ft (4–6 m)
Average weight:
500–1,000 lbs
(230–450 kg)

Body Count:
Total attacks: 21
Fatal attacks: 2

Distinguishing Characteristics:
Large size, flat rectangular head, prominent dorsal fin.

Habitat:
Continental shelves and lagoons in coastal, warm, temperate, and tropical waters

Diet:
Stingrays, fish, squid, octopus, crustaceans, other sharks and even their own young

Hunting Style:
The hammerhead swims directly above the ocean floor, swaying its flattened head from side to side in a sweeping motion to detect the electric signature of stingrays hiding beneath the sand. When a ray is located, the hammerhead delivers a hard blow from above, then pins it to the seafloor and chomps off each wing so it can't escape.

Natural Predators:
Larger hammerheads, bull sharks

Lifespan:
20–30 years

The uniquely shaped head is specially adapted to hunt the hammerhead's favorite meal: stingrays. The broad, flat area is densely packed with ampullae of Lorenzini—the sensory receptors all sharks use to detect the electromagnetic impulses of prey. The wide-set eye placement gives the hammerhead a greater range of vision to better scan the ocean floor for stingrays hiding in the sand.

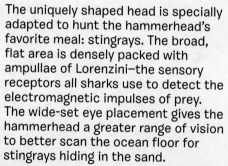

BLUE SHARK

(Prionace glauca)

With its indigo-colored back, vibrant blue sides, and white underbelly, the blue shark is one of the easiest sharks to identify. These sleek, fast, deep-water dwellers are likely responsible for the deaths of shipwreck and air crash victims. Naturally curious, they are known to circle swimmers or divers for 15 minutes or more.

Claim To Fame:
Best-looking shark

Size:
Average length:
6-10 ft (1.8-3 m)
Average weight:
60-120 lbs (27-54 kg)

Body Count:
Total attacks: 13*
Fatal attacks: 4
*Due to its deep, open-water habitat, blue sharks are likely responsible for the consumption of shipwrecked and downed-aircraft survivors. These multiple-casualty incidents are not included in global shark attack logs, so no one knows the actual human body count for the blue shark.

Distinguishing Characteristics:
Bright blue upper body; large eyes; long conical snout; very long, pointed pectoral fins

Habitat:
Deep waters of the world's temperate and tropical oceans

Diet:
Blue sharks prefer squid but will settle for fish, smaller sharks, and seabirds.

Hunting Style:
Like wolves, blue sharks are known to hunt in a cooperative pack. They work together to herd schools of fish into the shallows for easier feeding.

Natural Predators:
California sea lions, great whites, tiger shark, shortfin makos

Lifespan:
20+ years

BRONZE WHALER

(Carcharhinus brachyurus)

The name "whaler" dates back to the 19th century when these sharks would gather around the carcasses of harpooned whales hanging alongside whaling boats.

Claim to Fame:
The summer swimmer

Size:
Average length:
11 ft. (3.3 m)
Average weight:
672 lbs (305 kg)

Body Count:
Total attacks: 30
Fatal attacks: 1

Distinguishing Characteristics:
The bronze whaler's slim, streamlined body is a metallic olive-gray color with a pink tinge on the top and white on the bottom. The color darkens slightly toward the fin tips. It has a long, pointed snout and narrow, hook-shaped upper teeth.

Habitat:
Worldwide in warm, temperate, and subtropical waters and shallow coastline regions, freshwater and brackish areas of large rivers to shallow bays and estuaries

Diet:
Cephalopods, bony fish, cartilaginous fish

Hunting Style:
Bronze whalers hunt in groups up to 100.

Natural Predators:
Larger sharks

Lifespan:
25-30 years

SHORTFIN MAKO

(Isurus oxyrinchus)

With its dizzying speed, superb jumping abilities, and high intelligence, the mako is a fearsome predator. Reaching cruising speeds of 25 mph (40km) punctuated with bursts up to 46 mph (74 km), the mako can breach the water at heights of 30 ft (9 m) or higher! Angry makos have been known to attack and leap right into boats.

Claim to Fame:
Highest jumper

Size:
Average length:
10-12.5 ft (3-4 m)
Average weight:
672 lbs (305 kg)

Body Count:
Total attacks: 10
Fatal attacks: 1

Distinguishing Characteristics:
Makos have a brilliant, metallic-blue upper body. The shortfin mako can be identified by its white chin and snout. (Longfin makos have a blue chin and snout.)

Habitat:
Open water in temperate and tropical seas worldwide.

Diet:
Cephalopods, bony fish, other sharks, dolphins, seabirds

Hunting Style:
The mako swims below its prey, hovering in its blind spot, then suddenly lunges upward to capitalize on the element of surprise, often breaching the water.

Natural Predators:
Larger makos

Lifespan:
30 years

"Mako" is the Maori word for *shark.*

OCEANIC WHITETIP

(Carcharhinus longimanus)

Can you imagine surviving a shipwreck or plane crash into the ocean, only to be eaten by a shark? Thanks to the whitetip, many such "survivors" quickly become dinner. Like the blue shark, the whitetip lives in open water and is quick to arrive on the scene of a possible meal. Stubborn in their pursuit of prey, whitetips work themselves into a feeding frenzy as they compete for food.

Claim to Fame:
Frenzied feeder

Size:
Average length:
6–10 ft (2–3 m)
Average weight:
370 lbs (168 kg)

Body Count:
Total attacks: 10*
Fatal attacks: 3
*Due to its habit of eating sailors and others lost at sea, there is no accurate body count for the white tip because multiple-casualty incidents are not included in global shark attack logs.

Distinguishing Characteristics:
The whitetip's rounded fins and long, winglike pectoral and dorsal fins are easily identifiable. The fins have white tips that may be mottled.

Habitat:
Open water in temperate and tropical seas worldwide.

Diet:
Cephalopods, bony fish, other sharks, dolphins, seabirds

Hunting Style:
Whitetip feeding methods include biting into groups of fish and swimming through schools of tuna with an open mouth.

Though generally slow-moving, the whitetip will become aggressive in pursuit of prey. With the arrival of more whitetips at the scene, the competitors quickly work themselves into a vicious feeding frenzy.

Natural Predators:
Larger sharks

Lifespan:
Up to 22 years

During World War II, the Nova Scotia—a steamship carrying about 1,000 passengers—was sunk by a German submarine near South Africa. With only 192 survivors, many deaths were attributed to the whitetip.

ANATOMY OF A SHARK

Teeth

Shark teeth are attached to the gums rather than the jaw. Several backup rows exist so when a tooth is lost, another moves forward immediately to take its place. Shape depends on the shark's diet. Mollusk- and crustacean-eaters have blunt teeth for crushing; fish-eaters have thin, needlelike teeth to spear and grip; and meat-eaters have pointed, triangular-shaped teeth with tiny serrations for ripping through flesh.

Shape

Most shark bodies are rounded in the center and taper at each end like a bullet or torpedo, a hydrodynamic shape that increases speed.

Dermal Denticles

A shark's skin is made up of dermal denticles. These are tiny scales similar to teeth. Like teeth, each denticle has a layer of enamel and includes dentine and a pulp cavity. Denticles completely cover the shark's body and act as an external skeleton. Muscles are attached directly to the denticles, which makes them more efficient and saves energy. Denticles streamline the body to improve speed and provide protection from predators.

Fins

Most sharks have four to five fins:

Pectoral: Located near the head, the pectoral fins are used to lift and steer while swimming.

Pelvic: The pelvic fin sits behind the pectoral fin(s) and aids in stabilization.

Dorsal Fin: This is the fin that sticks out of the water when a shark swims close to the surface. It is also used for stabilization.

Anal Fin: Situated on the rear underside of the shark, these fins provide further stabilization.

Caudal Fin: Also called the tail fin, it provides the most thrust to propel the shark through the water. It has upper and lower lobes that vary in shape and size between types of shark. Most of the thrust comes from the top lobe.

Smell is the most important of a shark's senses. Sharks inhale water through their noistils and filter it through the olfactory sacs. Signals sent to the brain allow the shark to determine the presence of prey. It is said the great white can smell one drop of blood in 10 billion drops of water from more than 300 feet (91 m) away.

Gills

Like other fish, sharks breathe with gills instead of lungs. Water enters the shark's mouth and flows over the gills, where oxygen is absorbed into the bloodstream to be pumped throughout the body. The water then exits through five to seven gill slits on each side of the head.

Spiracles

Some sharks have openings above their eyes that draw oxygenated water into their gills. This means the shark can breathe while lying motionless on the sea floor. To keep water flowing over their gills, sharks without spiracles must move continuously.

Ampullae of Lorenzini

Small groups of sensitive cells under the skin in the shark's head detect the vibrations and electrical fields of fish and other prey.

Countershading

The upper half of the shark is dark to blend with the deeper water beneath when viewed from above. The lower half is white so it blends with the lighter water near the surface when viewed from below. This helps disguise the shark from predators and prey.

Nictitating Membrane

This translucent, tough membrane is a third eyelid that covers and protects the eye from damage during attacks. Not all sharks have them. The great white, for instance, must roll its eyes backward in their sockets for protection just before striking.

Lateral Line

This line of sensory cells along the shark's body detects changes in the movement of surrounding water. Erratic water movements indicate the presence of prey.

WHAT'S INSIDE

Skeleton

The skeleton of a shark is made of cartilage. This flexible connective tissue allows the shark to bend and twist easily. It is half the weight of bone, which lowers the shark's body mass, meaning less energy is used to propel it through the water.

Liver

A shark's liver is its largest internal organ. The liver stores a lot of oil, which provides an energy reserve between meals. Sharks have been known to survive on their internal oil as long as a year!

Digestion

Food moves from the mouth to the J-shaped stomach, where it can sit for long periods without being digested. Sharks will barf out undigestible items, but some species can completely turn the stomach inside out through their mouth, rinse it with seawater, and return it to its normal inside place.

A WORLD WITHOUT SHARKS

Despite a reputation as bloodthirsty man-eaters, sharks on average kill only three or four humans a year. Meanwhile, humans kill an estimated 100 million sharks each year–or 12,000 sharks per hour. Six thousand sharks were killed while you read this book.

Here are some of the reasons:

Overfishing:
Commercial fisheries harvest sharks for their meat and fins.

Sharkfin Soup:
An estimated 75 percent of sharks are killed each year for their fins alone. A symbol of wealth and prosperity, this traditional Chinese soup is served at weddings and special occasions. Because only the fin is valuable to hunters, it is sliced off, and the shark is thrown back into the ocean to die slowly from suffocation or a predatory attack. This horrific method is called *finning*.

Habitat Destruction:
Development and pollution push shark populations out of areas long used for feeding and nurseries.

Skin:
Shark leather is used for purses, bags, shoes, boots, coats, belts, wallets, car interiors, watch straps, gloves, gun holsters, and phone cases.

Bycatch:
Sharks become tangled in the nets, lines, trawls, and fish traps of commercial fisheries.

Sport Fishing and Trophy Hunting:
Due to their size, rarity, and fearsome reputation, sharks are greatly prized by trophy hunters.

Public Aquariums:
A live shark on display makes a lot of money for zoos and aquariums. Sadly, most captive sharks die within a year, even in the most state-of-the-art aquariums.

Public Fear:
Due to media exaggeration of sharks' threat to humans, the fear of sharks among the general population is so great, the mere sighting of a single shark can trigger an extensive cull (hunt) of the local shark population. Sharks also die from getting tangled in the shark barrier nets installed around swimming areas.

GLOSSARY

Apex predator—Predators with no natural predators of their own. They reside at the top of the food chain and have a crucial role in maintaining the health of their ecosystems.

Cartilaginous fish—Fish with a flexible skeleton made of cartilage instead of bone.

ISAF—International Shark Attack File

Serration—Jagged edges on a tooth that improve the ability to slice through meat